LifePrints

ESL FOR ADULTS

SECOND EDITION

1

Christy M. Newman

New Readers Press

LifePrints 1, 2nd edition
1-56420-310-7
Copyright © 2002
New Readers Press
U.S. Publishing Division of Laubach Literacy
1320 Jamesville Ave., Syracuse, New York 13210

Printed in the United States of America
9 8 7 6 5 4 3

Developmental Editor: Paula L. Schlusberg
Copy Editor: Judi Lauber
Production Director: Heather Witt
Designer: Shelagh Clancy
Cover Designer: Kimbrly Koennecke
Illustrators: Linda Tiff, Larry Raymond
Cover Illustrator: James P. Wallace
Production Specialists: Heather Witt, Alexander Jones

Series development by Robert Ventre, Inc./Course Crafters, Inc.

All proceeds from the sale of New Readers Press materials
support literacy programs in the United States and worldwide.

Table of Contents

1 2 3 4 5 6 7 8 9 10 11 12

Neighborhoods ■ ■ ■ ■ ■ ■ ■ ■ ■ ■ ■ ■

127 Center Street

At Home

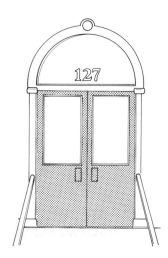

127 Center Street

Anita Gómez

Carol Wilson   Fred Wilson
                Kendra Wilson
                Michael Wilson

David Lin   Tom Lin
Lily Lin   May Lin

Where are you from?

I'm from _____.

Anita Gómez

David Lin   Lily Lin
Tom Lin   May Lin

Fred Wilson   Carol Wilson
Kendra Wilson   Michael Wilson

What language do you speak?

Around Town

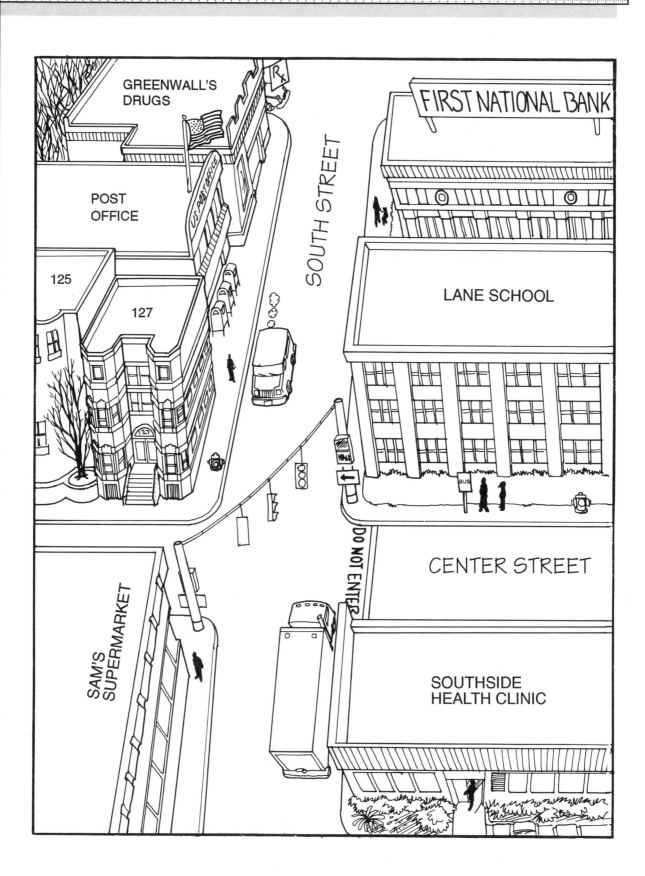

Check. ✔

There is …

			Yes	No
1		a supermarket.		
2		a school.		
3		a bank.		
4		a clinic.		
5		a drugstore.		
6		a post office.		
7				

In Town

Match.

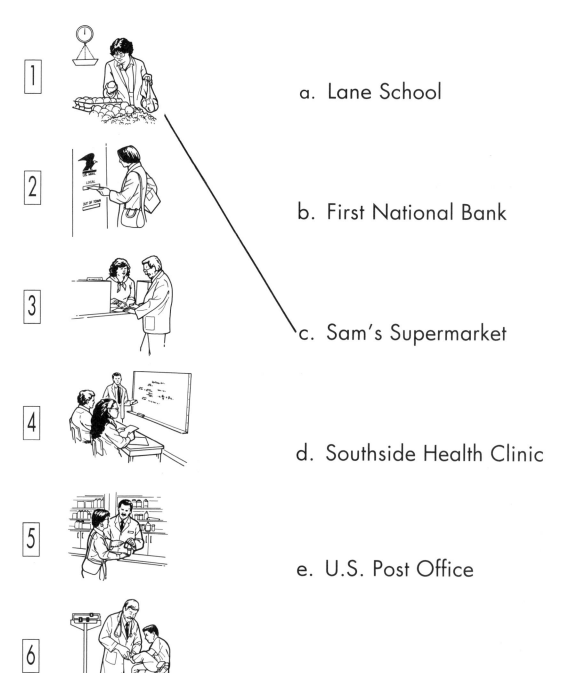

a. Lane School

b. First National Bank

c. Sam's Supermarket

d. Southside Health Clinic

e. U.S. Post Office

f. Greenwall's Drugs

Interview.

Name	Name	Name

Is there ...

1. a bank?			
2. a drugstore?			
3. a school?			
4. a post office?			
5. a supermarket?			
6. a clinic?			
7. ?			

On the Phone

Fred & Carol Wilson
883-0928
The Lin Family
884-4725
Southside Health Clinic
883-7500
Janet & Richard Stevens
(209) 762-2541

Copy.

1. Southside Health Clinic   8 8 3 – __ __ __ __

2. Janet and Richard Stevens   (__ __ __) 7 6 2 – 2 5 4 1

3. Fred and Carol Wilson   8 8 3 – __ __ __ __

4. The Lin family   __ __ __ – 4 7 2 5

What is your phone number?

My phone number is (__ __ __) __ __ __ – __ __ __ __ .

Health Check ✔

Emergency Services
Routine Health Care
No Appointments Necessary

7 Days a Week   900 Pleasant Street
24 Hours a Day   Evanston, IL 60211

(708) 765-1439

Fully Accredited Health Care Facility

CHICAGO MEDICAL CLINIC

• 24-hour Emergency Room

• Ambulance Service

2170 Porter Street   Chicago, IL 60602

788-9900

SOUTHSIDE HEALTH CLINIC

Emergency and Ambulatory Care
24 Hours a Day

555 South Street
Chicago, IL 60626

 883-7500

MIDTOWN HOSPITAL

• Health Care for Everyone
• Full Range of Services
• Outpatient Care

76 Hunt Street
(right off the Expressway, Exit 14)
Chicago, IL 60615

787-6000

Copy.   Telephone Numbers

1. Health Check   (_ _ _) _ _ _ – _ _ _ _

2. Chicago Medical Clinic   _ _ _ – _ _ _ _

3. Southside Health Clinic   _ _ _ – _ _ _ _

4. _____   _ _ _ – _ _ _ _

In an Emergency

1 Fire 2 Police 3 Ambulance

Fill in the form.

EMERGENCY INFORMATION

My name is _____.

I don't speak English. I speak _____.

My address is _____.

My apartment number is _____.

My phone number is ___ ___ ___ – ___ ___ ___ ___ .

NAME	PHONE
🔥 Fire	
🛡 Police	
✳ Ambulance	

Fill in the form.

(312) 884 – 4725   Chicago

Lily Lin   127 Center Street

60626   IL

IDENTIFICATION FORM
(Please print.)

NAME

ADDRESS

CITY	STATE	ZIP CODE

TELEPHONE NUMBER

I You We They	**live**	in Chicago.
He She It	**lives**	

Write *live* **or** *lives.*

1. The Wilsons _____ at 127 Center Street.

2. Anita _____ in apartment 1A.

3. Fred and Carol _____ in apartment 2A.

4. Lily Lin _____ in apartment 3A.

Answer *Yes, there is.* **or** *No, there isn't.*

1. Is there a supermarket? _____

2. Is there a clinic? _____

3. Is there a school? _____

4. Is there a bank? _____

	Pronoun	Verb *be*	Contraction
Singular (one)	I	am	I'm
	You	are	You're
	He She It	is	He's She's It's
Plural	You We They	are	You're We're They're

Write the pronoun. Then write the contraction.

Example: <u>**She**</u> is Anita Gómez. <u>**She's**</u> from Mexico.

1. _____ is Tom Lin. _____ from China.

2. _____ is May Lin. _____ also from China.

3. _____ are the Wilsons. _____ from Chicago.

4. My name is Michael. _____ from Chicago.

5. _____ are David and Lily Lin. _____ from China.

1 2 3 4 5 6 7 8 9 10 11 12

Families ■ ■ ■ ■ ■ ■ ■ ■ ■ ■ ■ ■

Janet and
Richard Stevens

Alma and
Harold Jones

Carol and Fred Wilson
Kendra and Michael

A Family Celebration

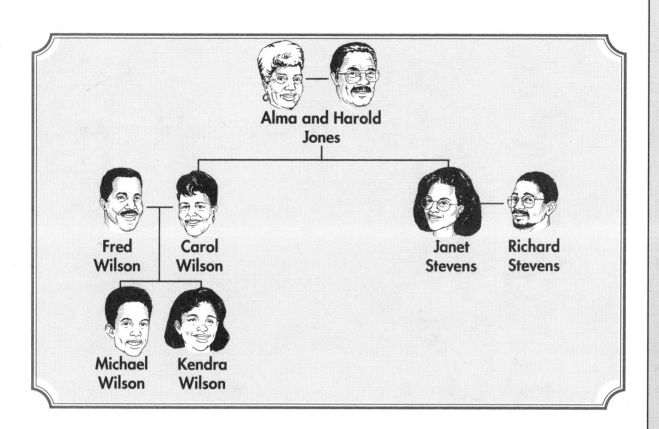

Copy.

Parents		Children	

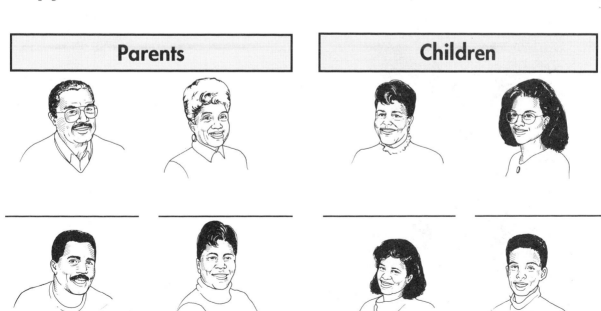

_____   _____   _____   _____

Family Members

Read.

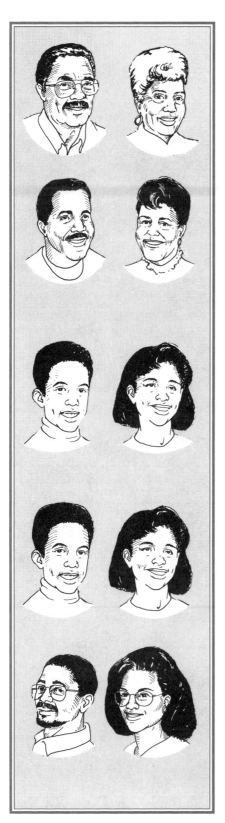

1. grandfather and grandmother

2. father and mother

3. son and daughter

4. brother and sister

5. husband and wife

Male or Female?

mother   son   grandmother   sister   father

brother   grandfather   wife   daughter   husband

Choose.

mother _____   son _____

_____   _____

_____   _____

_____   _____

_____   _____

Who's in the Family?

Check. ✔

	Carol	Fred	Kendra	Alma	Harold	Michael
1. mother	✔					
2. father						
3. sister	✔			░		
4. brother		░			░	
5. grand-father						
6. grand-mother						
7. husband						
8. wife	✔					
9. son						
10. daughter	✔					

Read.

Janet and Richard Stevens are visiting
Carol and Fred Wilson.
Janet and Carol are sisters.

Carol is planning a party
for Janet and Richard.
She's inviting family and friends.

Come to a Party!

For: Janet and Richard Stevens

Date: Saturday, October 2nd

Time: 8:00 p.m.

Place: 127 Center Street, Apt. 2A

Carol and Fred Wilson

Hello!

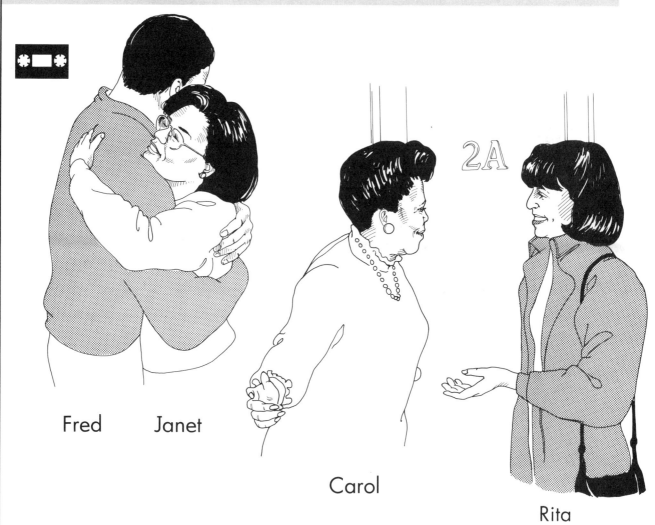

Fred   Janet

Carol

2A

Rita

Harold   Anita

Nice to Meet You

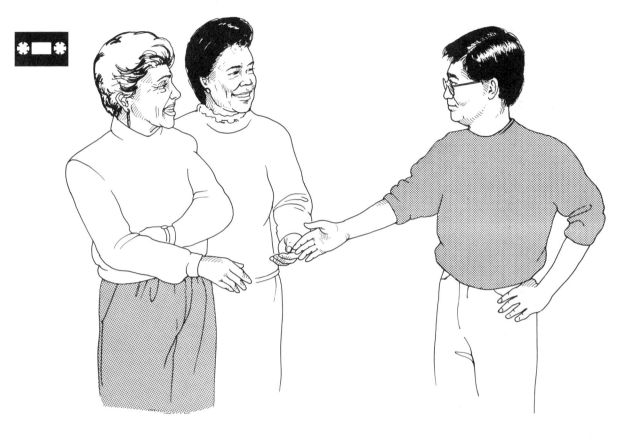

Alma   Carol   Tom

David   Lily   Fred   Richard

Days of the Week

Janet   Anita

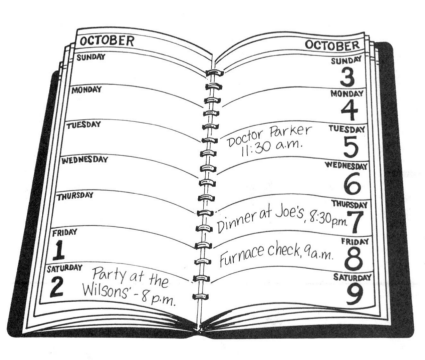

1. What day are Anita and Janet meeting for lunch?

    _____

2. What time are they meeting? _____

Janet and Richard Stevens are married.

Anita Gómez is single. She's not married.

Interview.

Name	Married	Single
1. Anita		✔
2. Janet	✔	
3.		
4.		
5.		

Are you married or single?

I'm _____.

Look Back

Read the form.

Your Name: Harold   Jones
                 First Name   Last Name

In Case of Emergency, Please Notify:

Alma   Jones
First Name   Last Name

(312) 884-7215   Wife
Telephone Number   Relationship

Fill in the form. Use your name.

Your Name: _____
                 First Name   Last Name

In Case of Emergency, Please Notify:

_____
First Name   Last Name

_____
Telephone Number   Relationship

September						
Sunday	Monday	Tuesday	Wednesday	Thursday	Friday	Saturday
					1	2
3	4	5	6	7	8	9
10	11	12	13	14	15	16

Write the day.

Example: Anita's birthday is September 6. It's on a ___**Wednesday**___.

1. Carol and Fred's anniversary is September 3.

    It's on a _____.

2. Alma is going to visit her sister from September 14 to September 16. She'll be there on _____, _____, and _____.

3. The Lins are having a party on September 11.

    It's on a _____.

4. Michael has a doctor's appointment on September 5.

    It's on a _____.

Write the date.

1. When is your birthday?   It's on _____.

2. When is New Year's Day?   It's on _____.

3. When is Thanksgiving?   It's on _____.

4. When is Labor Day?   It's on _____.

| No, I'm not. | No, he
No, she
No, it | isn't. | No, we
No, you
No, they | aren't. |

This is Fred Wilson's date book.

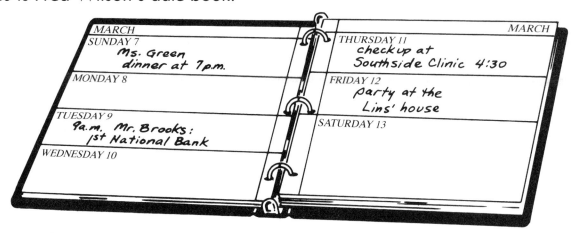

Write a negative answer.

Example: Kendra: Is Mr. Brooks at Southside Clinic?

Fred: _____**No, he isn't,**_____ Kendra. He's at the bank.

Kendra: Is your meeting at night?

Fred: _____. It's in the morning.

Kendra: Is the Lins' party on Sunday?

Fred: _____. The party is on Friday.

Kendra: Are Anita and Joe coming to the party?

Fred: _____. They have other plans.

Kendra: Are we going to Ms. Green's house?

Fred: _____. She's coming here.

1 2 **3** 4 5 6 7 8 9 10 11 12

Keeping in Touch ■ ■ ■ ■ ■ ■ ■ ■

Mrs. Wong

May Lin

Tom Lin

telephone operator

An International Call

 What's happening?

Long-Distance Information

Anita Gómez is calling her nephew, Arturo Soto.
Arturo lives in Brooklyn, New York.

Anita is dialing long-distance information.
She's dialing 1– 718–555–1212.

What's Arturo's phone number?

___ ___ ___ – ___ ___ ___ ___

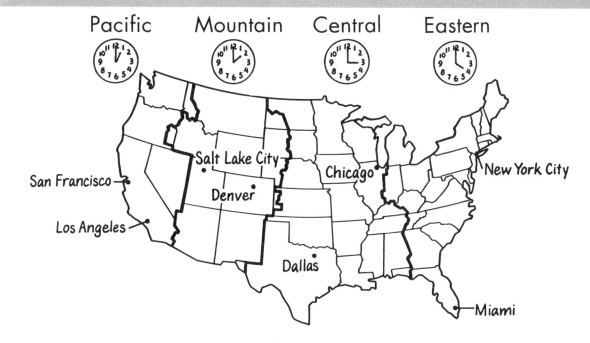

Pacific   Mountain   Central   Eastern

1. What is your time zone? _____

2. What time is it now?

3. What time is it in New York now?

4. What time is it in Dallas now?

5. What time is it in Denver now?

6. What time is it in San Francisco now?

Sending a Package

Address: Dr. Betty Walters
Southside Health Clinic

Phone: 883-7500

Address: Yu-lang Wong
27 Nanking Liu
Shanghai, China

Phone: 011-86-21-909-876

May Lin is sending a package to her mother.

Copy Mrs. Wong's address.

From:	May Lin
	127 Center Street
	Chicago, IL 60626
	U.S.A.

To: <u>Mrs. Yu-lang Wong</u>

_____

_____

_____

What's happening?

Post Office Sign

THE POST OFFICE IS CLOSED ON NOVEMBER 25.

Thursday, November 25, is a holiday.
The Post Office reopens on Friday, November 26.

HOURS

Monday – Friday:	8:00 a.m. – 5:00 p.m.
Saturday:	9:00 a.m. – 1:00 p.m.
Sundays and Holidays:	CLOSED

Check. ✔

			Open	Closed
1.	Sunday, November 21	10:00 a.m.		✔
2.	Monday, November 22	9:00 p.m.		
3.	Tuesday, November 23	9:00 a.m.		
4.	Wednesday, November 24	12:00 noon		
5.	Thursday, November 25	10:00 a.m.		
6.	Friday, November 26	8:30 a.m.		
7.	Saturday, November 27	4:30 p.m.		

Fill in the form.

UNITED STATES POSTAL MONEY ORDER			
00052736321	031109	60626	$ 25.00
SERIAL NUMBER	YEAR, MONTH, DAY	POST OFFICE	U.S. DOLLARS AND CENTS

PAY TO		
ADDRESS	FROM	Anita Gómez
	ADDRESS	127 Center St.
USED FOR		Chicago, IL 60626

⑁00008002⑁   0005273632⑊

Anita Gómez
127 Center St.
Chicago, IL 60626

Arturo Soto
1825 Hill Avenue
Brooklyn, NY 11201

Mailing a Package

May Lin is sending a package to her mother.
David Lin is helping her.
They are going to the wrong window.

Check. ✔

What is the right window?

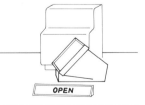

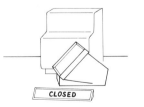

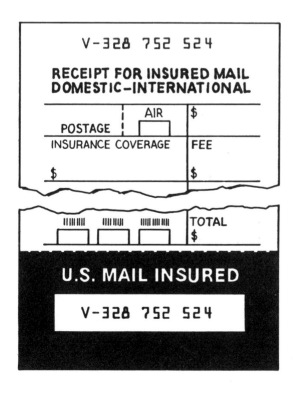

Fill in the form.

$20.50 $100.00 $2.40 $22.90

V-328 752 524

**RECEIPT FOR INSURED MAIL
DOMESTIC-INTERNATIONAL**

POSTAGE	AIR	$
INSURANCE COVERAGE		FEE
$		$

			TOTAL $

U.S. MAIL INSURED

V-328 752 524

Mailing Letters

Check. ✔

	Local	Out-of-Town	Foreign/Airmail
1 Mrs. Yu-lang Wong 27 Nanking Liu Shanghai China			
2 Arturo Soto 1825 Hill Avenue Brooklyn, NY 11201			
3 Marie Val 4 rue de Bal Port-au-Prince Haiti			
4 _____ _____ _____ _____			

Match.

You'd like to ...

1. send a letter to City Hall.

    a.

2. find out a phone number
    in another city.

    b.

    Local

3. mail a letter to El Salvador.

    c.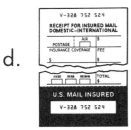

4. buy a money order.

    d.

5. insure a package to Germany.

    e.

    Foreign/Airmail

Full Form

I You He She It We You They	**would like to**	mail a letter.

Contraction

I You He She It We You They	**'d like to**	mail a letter.

Write the contraction. Then write about yourself.

Example: _____**I'd like to**_____ buy a stamp.

1. _____ send a package.

2. _____ buy money orders.

3. _____ find an address.

What would *you* like to do?

I'd like to _____.

I'd also like to _____.

Periods of Time	Days	Times on a Clock
in	**on**	**at**
the morning	Monday	1 o'clock
a while	Wednesday	6 p.m.
the winter	Sunday	2:30

Write *at* **or** *on.*

Janet: Can you meet me _____ Saturday?

Anita: Yes. Let's meet early. Can you meet

me _____ 8 a.m.?

Janet: That's too early. Let's meet _____ 10.

Anita: OK.

Janet: Thanks. I like to sleep late _____ weekends.

Write *in* **or** *on.*

Kendra: My class play is _____ Tuesday night.

Carol: Is the play _____ the evening?

Kendra: Yes, Mom. Will you go?

Carol: Of course. The whole family will go _____ Tuesday.

Kendra: It's a short play. We have school _____ the morning

_____ Wednesday.

1 2 3 4 5 6 7 8 9 10 11 12

Getting from Here to There ■ ■ ■ ■

Calling the Bus Company

What's happening?

Anita is calling the bus company.

She's asking directions to City Hospital.

Write the numbers you hear.

Bus number _____

$ _____

When does the next bus leave for City Hospital?

_____ : _____

To the Bus Stop

Anita wants to go to the bus stop.

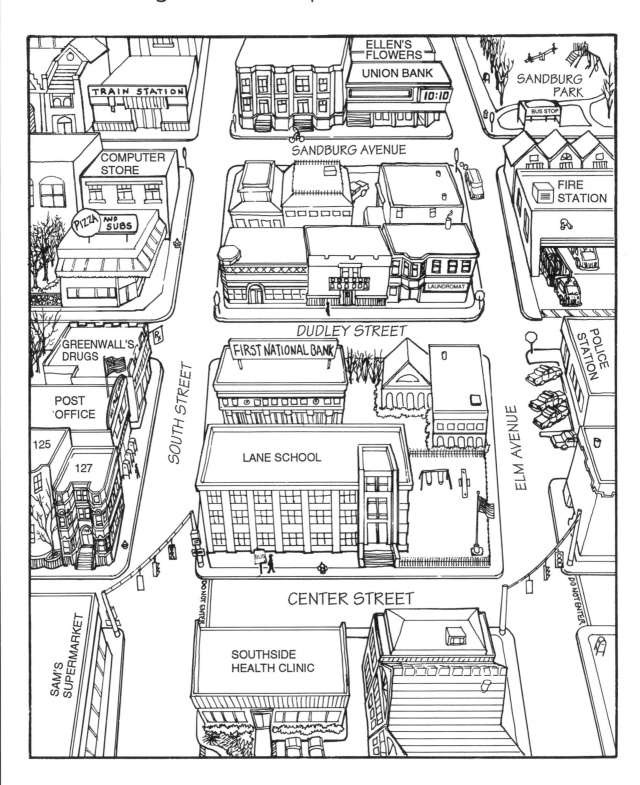

Bus 3 leaves:

Sandburg Park	Roper Square	City Hospital
10:00 a.m.	10:15	10:30
10:30	10:45	11:00
11:00	11:15	11:30
11:30	11:45	12:00

Complete the sentences.

1. The next bus leaves Sandburg Park at _____ : _____.

2. Bus 3 leaves Roper Square every _____ minutes.

3. Anita arrives at City Hospital at _____ : _____.

On the Bus

Look.

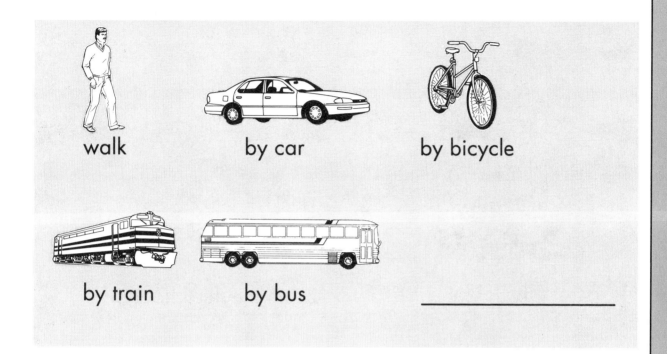

walk   by car   by bicycle

by train   by bus   _____

Interview.

How do you get to class?

Name	walk	by car	by bus	by train	by bicycle	other
1. Michael Wilson	✔					
2.						
3.						
4.						
5.						

Finding the Right Room

1. across the lobby

2. on the third floor

3. down the hall

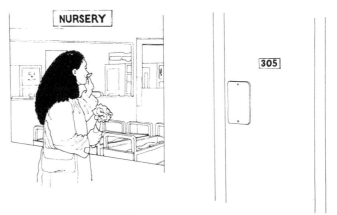

4. next to the nursery

5. in room 305

across   down   in   next to   on

Complete the sentences.

1. The flowers are _____ the table.

2. The baby is _____ Sonia's arms.

3. The nurse is walking _____ the hall.

4. Sonia is _____ _____ the window.

5. Room 306 is _____ the hall.

Getting Around

walk

car

bus

train

_____

bicycle

How do you go to ...

	Native country	Here
1. school?		
2. work?		
3. the store?		
4. the post office?		
5. the hospital?		
6. ?		

Interview.

Name	What Country ... ?	How ... ?
1. Anita Gómez	Mexico	by bus
2. Tom Lin	China	by train, by plane
3.		
4.		
5.		
6.		

Look Back

| in the shop | across the street | next to the bank |
| down the street | on a bicycle |

Complete the sentences.

1. Anita is buying flowers _____.

2. Sandburg Park is _____ from Ellen's Flower Shop.

3. The fire station is _____ from the park.

4. Ellen's Flower Shop is _____.

5. Kendra is _____.

I'm You're He's She's It's We're They're	calling	information.

Write the contraction and verb.

Example: Carol is on the phone. __She's calling__ information.
(she/call)

1. The operator asks for a name and address.

   _____ up the number.
   (he/look)

2. Carol phones her family. _____ for her call.
   (they/wait)

3. She dials the number. _____.
   (it/ring)

Check ✔ the sentences that tell Fred what to do.

Example: _____ How do I find room 509?

   __✔__ First, go down the hall.

_____ Then take the elevator to the fifth floor.

_____ On the fifth floor, do I go left or right?

_____ Turn left and walk to the end of the hall.

_____ That's where room 509 is.

_____ Please knock before you go in.

Write the correct preposition: *across, at, down, near,* **or** *next to.*

Example: Where is Anita?   She's ___**at**___ the bus stop.

1. Where is the bus?   It's _____ the bus stop.

2. Where is the fire hydrant?   It's _____ the street.

3. Where are the man and woman?   They're _____ Anita.

4. Where is the clock?   It's _____ the street.

Begin the questions with *Where* **or** *How.*

Question	Answer
1. _____ is the train to Portland?	On Wilder Street.
2. _____ far is that from Union Bank?	Two blocks south.
3. _____ much is the fare?	$4.25.
4. _____ can I buy a ticket?	On the train.

1 2 3 4 5 6 7 8 9 10 11 12

Feelings ■ ■ ■ ■ ■ ■ ■ ■ ■ ■ ■ ■

Feeling Good, Feeling Bad

What's happening?

Our Feelings

How do they feel?

1. happy

_____

_____

2. sad

_____

_____

3. afraid

_____

_____

4. angry

_____

_____

angry	joyful	afraid
happy	upset	glad
scared	sad	unhappy

1. _____

2. _____

3. _____

4. _____

Thinking of Home

Answer the questions.

1. How does Anita feel?

2. Why?

3. What can she do?

Answer the questions.

1. How does May feel?

2. Why?

3. How does the mail carrier feel?

4. Why?

Talking to Friends

Answer the questions.

1. What's happening?

2. How does Fred feel?

Good News

Answer the questions.

1. What's the good news?

2. How does Michael feel?

3. How does Kendra feel?

4. How do Carol and Fred feel?

Everyone has good days.
Everyone has bad days.

Michael feels good today.
He is happy and proud.

Anita feels bad today.
She is sad and lonely.

Interview.

What makes you feel good?
What makes you feel bad?

Name	Good	Bad
1.		
2.		
3.		
4.		

What's the Matter?

Answer the questions.

1. How does Kendra feel?

2. Why?

3. What makes you feel angry?

| glad | afraid | angry |
| happy | joyful | upset |

Write the words that mean you're feeling:

good	**bad**

Verbs: Present: *Be* and *Do*

	Verb: *Be*	Verb: *Do*
I	am	do
He She It	is	does
We You They	are	do

Write the correct form of *be*.

Example: "Alma and Harold __are__ my parents," says Janet.

1. "Carol and I _____ sisters, too."

2. "I _____ from Brooklyn," says Arturo.

3. "But Aunt Anita _____ from Mexico."

4. Where _____ you from?

Write *is/are* **or** *do/does*.

Question	Answer
Example: How __is__ Anita? How __does__ Anita feel?	She's happy. She feels happy.
1. How _____ Harold feel?	He feels upset.
2. How _____ Janet and Richard?	They're very happy.
3. How _____ Sonia?	She's fine.
4. How _____ Alma and Harold feel?	They feel lonely.

Present	
I	laugh.
He She It	laughs.
You We They	laugh.

Present Continuous	
I	am laughing.
He She It	is laughing.
You We They	are laughing.

What are they doing? How do they feel?
Complete the sentences. Then write about yourself.

Example: May _____ **is standing** _____ behind the door.
(stand)

She _____ **feels** _____ afraid.
(feel)

1. Kendra _____ to Michael.
(listen)

2. She _____ angry and sad.
(feel)

3. Anita _____ Sonia.
(visit)

4. They _____ happy.
(feel)

What are *you* doing? I _____.

How do *you* feel? I _____.

Pronouns and Verb: *Be*

Pronouns

Singular (one)	*Plural* (two or more)
I you he she it	we you they

Verb: *Be*

I	**am.**	(I'm)
He She It	**is.**	(He's) (She's) (It's)
We You They	**are.**	(We're) (You're) (They're)

Underline the pronoun.

1. Anita Gómez is from Mexico.

   She speaks English and Spanish.

2. Fred Wilson is from the United States.

   He speaks English.

3. Tom and May Lin are from China.

   They speak Chinese.

Write the pronoun.

Arturo Soto lives in New York. _____ is Anita's nephew.

Anita asks, "Are _____ coming to Chicago?"

Arturo answers, "Yes, _____ am coming next month."

Yes/No **with** *Be*		
Am	I	
Is	he she it	working?
Are	you we they	from New York?

Yes/No **with** *Do*		
Do	I you we they	work?
Does	he she it	

Begin the question with *Is* or *Are*.

1. _____ Fred and Carol Wilson from Chicago?
2. _____ Janet Stevens visiting them?

3. _____ May Lin from China?
4. _____ Kendra and Michael her children?

Begin the question with *Do* or *Does*.

Janet: "I'm going to Mexico City. _____ your mother live there?"

Anita: "Yes. She lives with my brother. _____ you want their address?"

Janet: "Yes, thanks. _____ they speak English?"

Anita: "No. _____ your husband speak Spanish?"

Question	Answer
Who? **What?** **Where?**	person thing place

Question	Answer
When? **Why?** **How?**	time reason way

Question

Answer

Who lives in Apartment 1A?

Anita Gómez

What language does she speak?

Spanish

Where does she live?

127 Center Street

Match the questions and answers.

1. **When** does Michael go to school?   a.

2. **How** does he get there?   b.

3. **Why** is Michael happy?   c.

The pictures are the answers. Make up the questions.

Present

I You We They	**work.**
He She It	**works.**

Present Continuous

I	**am working.**
He She It	**is working.**
You We They	**are working.**

Identify the sentences.

	Present	Present Continuous
Example: Fred is talking to Michael.	_____	✔
1. Carol is writing invitations.	_____	_____
2. Arturo lives in Brooklyn.	_____	_____
3. Kendra and Michael are going to school.	_____	_____
4. Sonia is having a baby.	_____	_____
5. Tom Lin speaks English and Chinese.	_____	_____
6. Alma and Harold have two daughters.	_____	_____

What's happening? Make up the sentences.

Possessives

Possessives

Singular	Plural	
My	Our	
Your	Your	
His (Tom's)	Their (Tom and May's)	address is 127 Center Street.
Her (May's)	(The Lins')	
Its		

Tom is **Lily's** father. Tom is **her** father.

Lily is **David's** sister. Lily is **his** sister.

Tom is **Lily and David's** father.

Tom is **their** father.

Match.

1. Fred's children   a. our children

2. Fred and Carol's children   b. his children

3. your children and my children   c. her children

4. Alma's children   d. their children

Write the correct possessive.

Carol: "This is Tom Lin. May is _____ wife. They have two children."

Janet: "Are Lily and David _____ children?"

Carol: "Yes. May's mother lives in China. May calls _____ mother often."

1 2 3 4 5 6 7 8 9 10 11 12

What Did You Do Before? ■ ■ ■ ■ ■

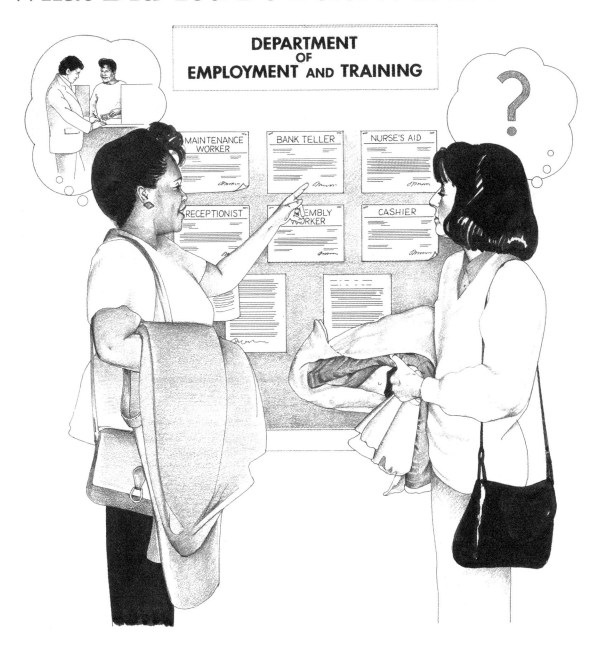

Looking for Work

📼 What's happening?

Different Jobs

Bank Teller
First National Bank
20 hrs./wk.
Health plan
$12.00–$15.00/hr.

Maintenance Worker
Danner Stores
7 a.m.–3 p.m.; 3 p.m.–11 p.m.; or
11 p.m.–7 a.m.
No benefits
$8.50/hr.

Nurse's Aide
Memorial Hospital
No benefits
Part-time: 5 p.m.–10 p.m.
$8.50–$12.00/hr.

Receptionist
Southside Health Clinic
Full-time, days
Health, dental, vacations
$325.00–$400.00/wk.

Assembly Worker
Coleman Electronics Inc.
8 a.m.–4 p.m.
Health plan
$350.00–$475.00/wk.

Cashier
24-Hour Market
No benefits
Night shift: 11 p.m.–7 a.m.
$12.00/hr.

Complete and check. ✔

Job Title	Employer	Salary		Hours		Benefits	
		Weekly	Hourly	Full-time	Part-time	Yes	No
1. Bank Teller	First National Bank		✔		✔	✔	
2. Maintenance Worker							
3. Nurse's Aide							
4. Receptionist							
5. Assembly Worker							
6. Cashier							

In Line

Read the form.

Department of Employment and Training

Full Name: <u>Margarita Elena Pérez</u>   Date of Birth: <u>December 21, 1978</u>

Address: <u>125 Center Street, Apt. 4</u>

<u>Chicago, IL 60626</u>

Telephone Number: <u>(312) 883-0908</u>

U.S. Citizen: Yes ____ No <u>X</u>

Country of Origin: <u>El Salvador</u>

Social Security Number: <u>639-99-2693</u>

Check Highest Grade Completed:

____ Elementary   ____ Jr. High School   <u>X</u> High School

____ College   ____ Graduate School   ____ Other _____

Date: <u>January 18, 2004</u>   Signature: <u>Margarita Pérez</u>

A-H   I-P   Q-Z

_____ _____ _____

_____ _____ _____

Fill in the form. Use your name.

Department of Employment and Training

Full Name: _____ Date of Birth: _____

Address: _____

_____

Telephone Number: _____

U.S. Citizen: Yes _____ No _____

Country of Origin: _____

Social Security Number: _____

Check Highest Grade Completed:

____ Elementary   ____ Jr. High School   ____ High School

____ College   ____ Graduate School   ____ Other _____

Date: _____ Signature: _____

Getting Advice

Choose the correct answer.

1. Where did Rita come from?	El Salvador	Mexico
2. Did she finish high school?	yes	no
3. Where did she work?	in a factory	in a hospital
4. Did she like her work?	yes	no
5. Where did she learn English?	at work	at Lane School

1. Tom was a farmer.

2. Anita was a student.

3. Rita was a factory worker.

What did you do in your native country?

I was a _____.

Making Choices

| home | full-time | Spanish and English | night | people |

Complete the sentences.

1. Rita speaks _____.

2. She likes to work with _____.

3. She'd like to work near her _____.

4. She'd like to work _____.

5. Sometimes she can work at _____.

Your Choice

What kind of work would you like?

Check. ✔

	Yes	No
Would you like ...		
1. full-time work?		
2. part-time work?		
3. outdoor work?		
4. indoor work?		
5. day work?		
6. night work?		

Your Past, Present, and Future

Interview.

Name	I was ...	Now I am ...	I'd like to be ...
1. Carol Wilson	a cashier.	not working.	a bank teller.
2. Tom Lin	a farmer.	a store manager.	a store owner.
3. Anita Gómez	a student.	a superintendent.	an electrician.
4.			
5.			
6.			
7.			

Match.

1. assembly worker

a.

2. cashier

b.

3. receptionist

c.

4. maintenance worker

d.

5. bank teller

e.

6. nurse's aide

f.

Prepositions of Place

in	a factory a supermarket a repair shop	on	a farm an assembly line a truck

Prepositions of Time

during in at	the day the afternoon night

Complete the sentences.

1. Rita can work _____ night.

2. Carol wanted to work _____ a bank.

3. She likes to work _____ the day.

4. Tom worked _____ a farm.

Singular

I He She It	was wasn't	a student.

Plural

We You They	were weren't	students.

Write *was* or *were*.

1. Rita _____ a student.

2. Carol and May _____ cashiers.

3. Arturo _____ a factory worker.

Write *wasn't* or *weren't*.

1. Arturo and Rita _____ happy in a factory.

2. May _____ a farmer in China.

| I
He
She
It
We
You
They | work**ed**

didn't work | on a farm. |

Complete the sentences.

Example: Rita _____**worked**_____ in a factory.
(work)

She _____***didn't live***_____ on a farm.
(not live)

1. Rita _____ to a job counselor.
(talk)

2. She _____ where to apply.
(not know)

3. She _____ to work in a factory
(not want)
again.

Department of Employment and Training

4. Rita _____ the application form.
(complete)

5. She _____ any blank spaces.
(not leave)

6. Rita _____ her full name.
(sign)

1 2 3 4 5 6 7 8 9 10 11 12

The Cost of Things ■ ■ ■ ■ ■ ■ ■

Mrs. Lin's Birthday

What's happening?

Great Values! Great Values! Great Values! Great Values!

1/2 Price Sale Day at Danner Stores!

For Her

Watches $50
Now $25

Slippers $22
Now $11

For Him

Pants $42
Now $21

Shirts $30
Now $15

For the Kids

T-shirts $12
Now $6

Sneakers $28
Now $14

All toys 1/2 price!

What do you want for your birthday?

The Store Directory

Children

clothes .... 2nd floor
shoes ....2nd floor
toys .... basement

Housewares

home appliances ....basement
lamps .... basement
linens .... 2nd floor

Men

coats .... 3rd floor
shirts .... 3rd floor
shoes .... main floor
suits .... 3rd floor

Women

accessories ..... main floor
dresses .... 2nd floor
jewelry .... main floor
shoes .... main floor
sweaters .... main floor

What can you buy ...

in the basement?	on the main floor?	on the 2nd floor?	on the 3rd floor?

David and Lily have $12.00.

What can they buy?

_____   _____   _____

In the Shoe Department

How much are the slippers that are on sale? _____

What are the colors of the slippers?

_____ _____ _____

Danner Stores

2/5/04

Slippers	11.00
Tax	.96
TOTAL	11.96
Cash Tend.	12.00
Change	.04

Thank you!

Complete the sentences.

1. The slippers cost _____ in total.

2. The tax on the slippers was _____ .

3. Lily gave the clerk _____ .

4. The clerk gave Lily _____ in change.

Sizes

Check. ✔

	Small (S)	Medium (M)	Large (L)
1			✔
2			
3			
4			
5			
6			

Mr. Lin went to the department store.
He wanted to buy a present.

Does Mr. Lin want help now?   Yes   No

Mr. Lin looked at the sign.
The salesclerk told him the price
and showed him a watch.

Special
50% off
Watches Now
$25.00

How much do the watches usually cost? $50 $25

Writing Checks

	278
THOMAS LIN 127 CENTER ST. CHICAGO, IL 60626	_February 5,_ _2004_

PAY TO THE ORDER OF _Danner Stores_ $ | 27.19 |

Twenty seven and _¹⁹/₁₀₀_ ———————— DOLLARS

UNION BANK

MEMO _____   _Thomas Lin_

⑆ 221271346 ⑈ 4672 926772 ⑉ 0278

Pay this amount by check.

279

PAY TO THE
ORDER OF _____ $ [   ]

_____ DOLLARS

UNION BANK

MEMO _____

⑆221271346⑆ 4672 926772⑈ 0278

Look Back

May Lin got some presents for her birthday.
She liked them all.

What did May get for her birthday?

1. _____ slippers   5. _____ shoes

2. _____ suit   6. _____ dress

3. _____ hat   7. _____ sweater

4. _____ coat   8. _____ toys

What else did May get? _____

Question	Answer
What?	thing
When?	time

Question	Answer
Where?	place
How?	way

Question	Answer
Who?	person

Write *Who, What, Where,* **or** *When.*

Question	Answer
Example: __Who?__	Alma Jones.
1. _____?	On Monday.
2. _____?	In a department store.
3. _____?	Sizes 10 and 12.
4. _____?	During the day.
5. _____?	On a farm.
6. _____?	Lily and David.
7. _____?	Many colors.

Write the question word.

Question	Answer
1. _____ do Lily and David buy?	A present.
2. _____ does Mr. Lin find watches?	On the main floor.
3. _____ is Mrs. Lin's birthday?	On Tuesday.
4. _____ does Mrs. Lin feel about her birthday?	Very happy.

Questions: *How much* / Verbs: *Need, Want*

Singular	Plural
How much does the shirt **cost?**	**How much do** the shirts **cost?**
How much is the shirt?	**How much are** the shirts?

Write the questions.

Question	**Answer**
Example: <u>How much does the sweater cost?</u>	The sweater costs $25.
1. _____	The sneakers are $35.
2. _____	Umbrellas cost $18.
3. _____	The hat is $15.75.

Pronoun	Verb		
I You We They	**need** **want**	to eat to buy	breakfast every morning. a fancy car.
He She	**needs** **wants**	to eat to buy	breakfast every morning. a fancy car.

Write the correct form of *need* **or** *want.*

Example: It's Mrs. Lin's birthday. Her husband <u>**wants**</u> to buy a watch for her. He's paying by check. He <u>**needs**</u> to sign his name on it.

1. David and Lily _____ to buy slippers for their mother.

2. The slippers are $11. David and Lily _____ to pay the tax, too.

3. Lily _____ to get a pink shirt. She _____ size 7.

1 2 3 4 5 6 7 8 9 10 11 12

Getting Well ■ ■ ■ ■ ■ ■ ■ ■ ■ ■ ■ ■

In the Waiting Room

What's Happening?

The Human Body

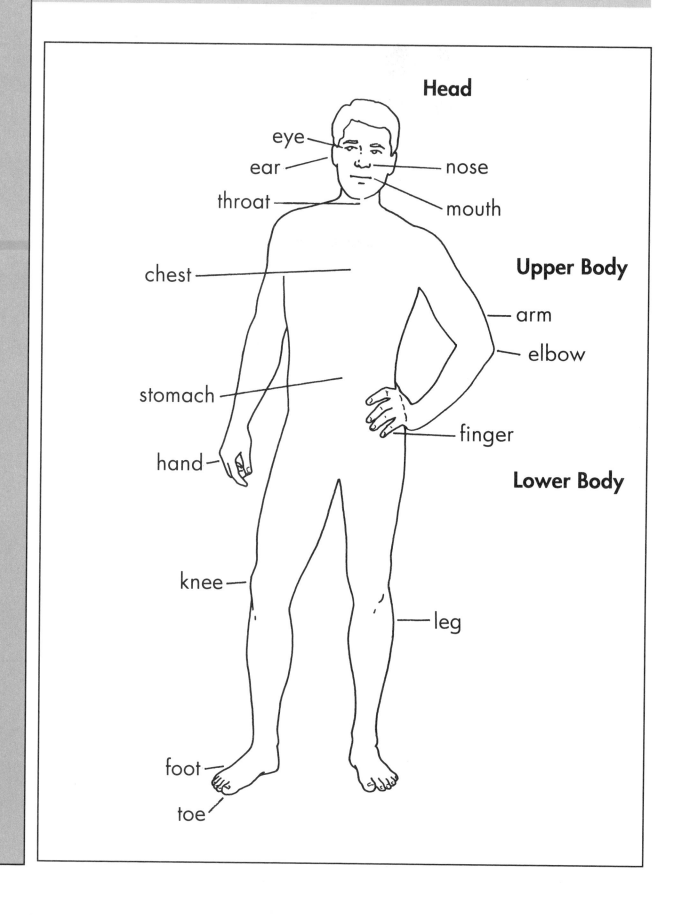

Head

eye

ear

throat

nose

mouth

chest

Upper Body

arm

elbow

stomach

finger

hand

Lower Body

knee

leg

foot

toe

Check. ✔

	Ear	Head	Leg	Nose	Stomach	Throat
1				✔		
2						
3						
4						
5						
6						

Health Insurance Form

HEALTH USA/Family Plan
P.O. Box 5002
Chicago, IL 60212

GROUP INSURANCE IDENTIFICATION CARD

NAME
WILSON, FRED
POLICY
566985-001

Fred Wilson

EMPLOYEE'S SIGNATURE

Fill in the form.

 SOUTHSIDE HEALTH CLINIC

Patient's Name: <u>Kendra Wilson</u>   Date: <u>March 3, 2004</u>

Address: <u>127 Center Street</u>

<u>Chicago, IL 60626</u>

Telephone: <u>883-0928</u>

Health Insurance: _____ Yes   _____ No

Name of Insurance Company: _____

Address: _____

_____

Policy or Group Number: _____

Name of Employee: _____

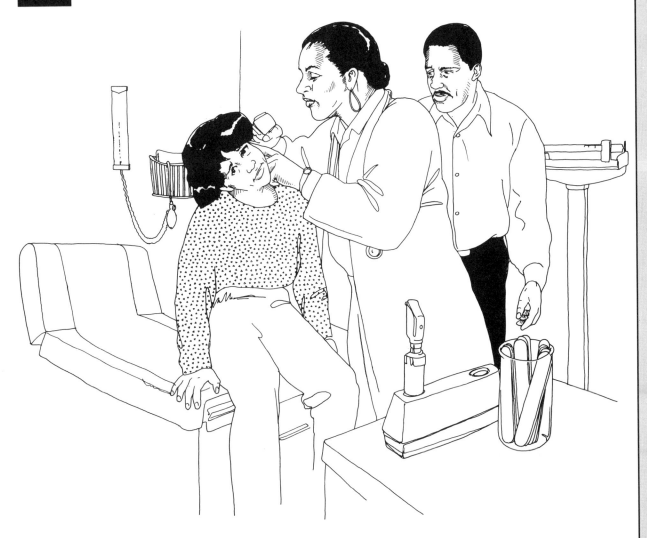

What's wrong with Kendra?

____ fever   ____ headache   ____ earache

____ sore throat   ____ stomachache   ____ stuffed-up nose

Doctor's Advice

Kendra has the flu. She has
an ear infection too.

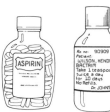

She can take aspirin
for the fever. She can take
an antibiotic for the infection.

Kendra needs to rest
and drink lots of liquids.

Kendra can go back
to school soon.

Choose the correct answer.

1. What's wrong with Kendra?	flu	stomachache
2. What kind of infection does she have?	ear	eye
3. What can she take for the infection?	aspirin	antibiotic

I have an earache. My throat hurts too.

I have a broken arm.

What would you say?

1

2

3

4

5

6

At the Drugstore

Read the labels.

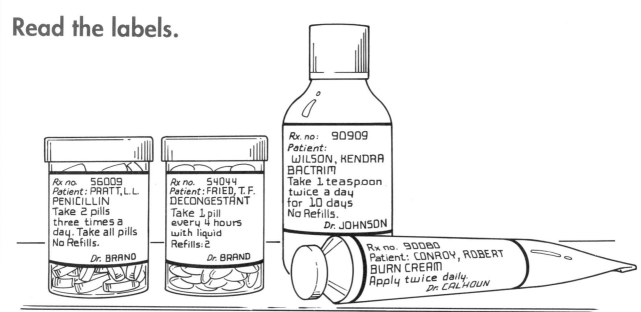

Rx no. 56009
Patient: PRATT, L.L.
PENICILLIN
Take 2 pills
three times a
day. Take all pills
No Refills.
Dr. BRAND

Rx no. 54044
Patient: FRIED, T.F.
DECONGESTANT
Take 1 pill
every 4 hours
with liquid
Refills: 2
Dr. BRAND

Rx no: 90909
Patient:
WILSON, KENDRA
BACTRIM
Take 1 teaspoon
twice a day
for 10 days
No Refills.
Dr. JOHNSON

Rx no. 90080
Patient: CONROY, ROBERT
BURN CREAM
Apply twice daily.
Dr. CALHOUN

Complete the chart.

Patient	Medicine	Amount	Times Daily	Special Directions
1. Wilson, Kendra		I teaspoon		take for 10 days
2.	Burn cream			
3.	Decongestant		6	
4.		2 pills	3	

Absence Notes

March 14, 2004

Dear Ms. Brown,

My daughter, Kendra, had the flu last week. She had a fever and an earache.

Carol Wilson

Write an absence note to your child's teacher.

Dear _____ ,

_____

_____

_____

_____

directions   health problems   body parts

Write the category.

1 | take twice a day   apply daily   take with food

_____

2 | sore throat   earache   broken arm

_____

3 | 2 pills   1 teaspoon   1 tablet

_____

4 | elbow   hand   finger

_____

5 | headache   fever   infection

_____

Verbs: Present

I	am feel	
He She It	is feels	sick. fine. cold.
We You They	are feel	

I	have	
He She It	has	a cold. a headache. a broken leg.
We You They	have	

Write *is/are* **or** *have/has.*

Anita: Hi, Carol. How are you?

Carol: I'm fine. But Tom Lin _____ the flu.

Anita: I'm sorry to hear that. How _____ his children?

Carol: They _____ sick, too. Lily _____ a fever and chills.
David _____ a bad cough.

Anita: That's terrible. How _____ your family?

Carol: We _____ all fine.

Write *have/has* **or** *feel/feels.*

1. You need a cast. You _____ a broken ankle.

2. She should go to the dentist. She _____ a toothache.

3. She has a bad cold. She _____ terrible.

4. I need a bandage. I _____ a cut on my hand.

5. Give me some cough syrup. My throat _____ sore.

6. They're staying home today. They _____ sick.

Past Tense Verbs

I He She It We You They	had	a cold.
	felt	sick.

Past Time Words

last	ago	yesterday
last night	a few minutes ago	yesterday morning
last weekend	an hour ago	yesterday afternoon
last Monday	a week ago	yesterday evening
last month	a month ago	
last year	a year ago	

Write *had* **or** *felt.*

Example: He ___**had**___ a headache yesterday.

1. She _____ an upset stomach last week.

2. Kendra _____ an earache last week.

3. She _____ better after a few days.

Identify the sentences.

	Present	Past
Example: Lily often has a cold in the winter.	✔	_____
1. She and David were sick every day last week.	_____	_____
2. Carol had a cough this morning.	_____	_____
3. Now she feels better.	_____	_____
4. The Lins and the Wilsons are much better now.	_____	_____

1 2 3 4 5 6 7 8 9 10 11 12

Asking for Help ■ ■ ■ ■ ■ ■ ■

A Kitchen Fire

What's happening?

1. What's the emergency telephone number?

_____

2. What's the emergency telephone number in your area?

_____

More about the Fire

There was a fire at 127 Center Street. It started in Apartment 2A. Fred Wilson burned his dinner. Then the curtains caught on fire.

Anita Gómez called 911 for help. The fire fighters came and put out the fire.

Check. ✔

	True	False
1. There was a fire in Apartment 2B.		
2. Fred's dinner burned.		
3. The curtains caught on fire.		
4. Anita called the police.		
5. The fire fighters didn't put out the fire.		

home   kitchen   work   curtains   living room

Complete the sentences.

1. The fire started in the _____.

2. The _____ caught on fire.

3. Fred was in the _____.

4. Tom and May were at _____.

5. Carol was at _____.

After the Fire

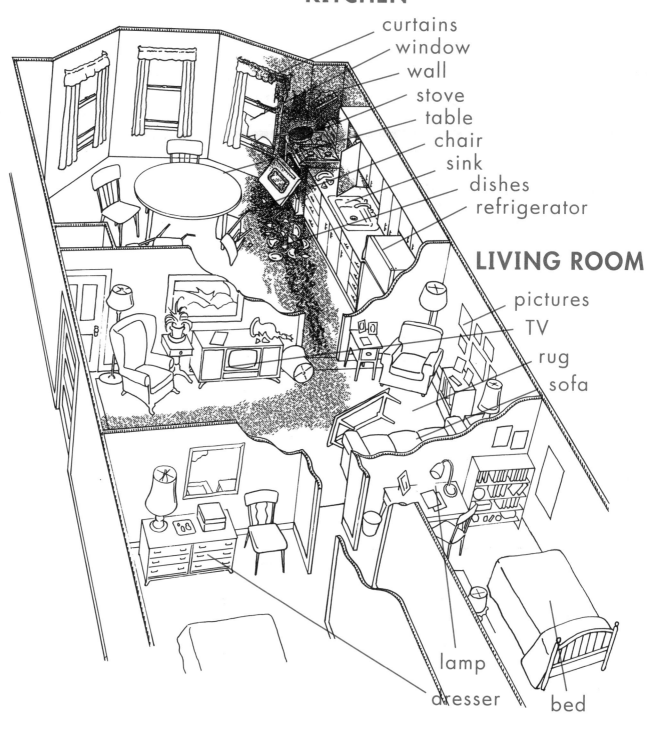

KITCHEN
curtains
window
wall
stove
table
chair
sink
dishes
refrigerator

LIVING ROOM
pictures
TV
rug
sofa

lamp
dresser
bed

BEDROOM

table   bed   chair   stove   lamp   coffee table

rug   sofa   TV   sink   dresser   bookcase

Where would you put it?

Kitchen	Living Room	Bedroom

Making Repairs

curtains   rugs   walls   stove   window

Complete Anita's work list.

1. call <u>electric company</u>

2. replace _____

3. fix _____

4. paint _____

5. clean _____

What will Fred buy?

_____

What's the problem?

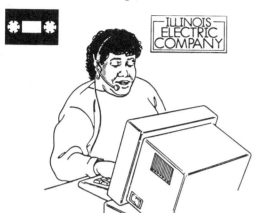

1. _____

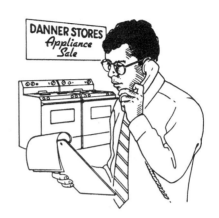

2. _____

3. _____

4. _____

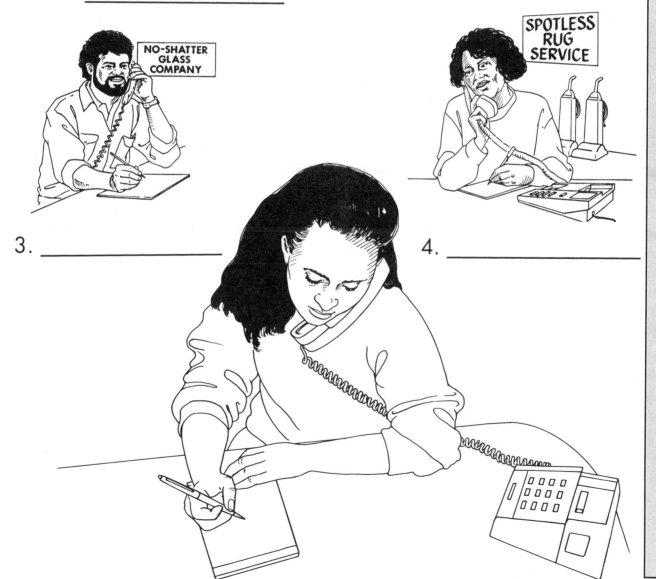

About You

Here are some common problems in the home:

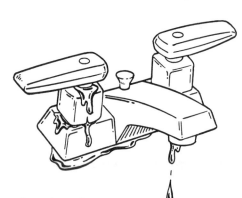

1. leaky faucet

2. broken stairs

3. peeling paint

4. broken doorknob

What needs to be fixed at your house?

_____   _____

_____   _____

_____   _____

_____   _____

April 23, 2004

Dear Anita,
   We have many problems from the fire in 2A. Our kitchen walls are black from the smoke. The ceiling is dirty too. Our kitchen lights don't work. When can you fix these problems?

Sincerely,
Tom Lin
Apt. 3A

What needs to be fixed at your house?
Write a letter to your landlord.

_____

Dear _____ ,

_____

_____

_____

_____

_____

       Sincerely,

_____

Look Back

Complete the sentences.

1

Paint the _____.

2

Fix the _____.

3

Clean the _____.

4

Replace the _____.

5

Clean the _____.

6

Replace the _____.

The window is **peeling.**

 The window is **painted.**

Underline the participle. Then check ✔ *True or False.*

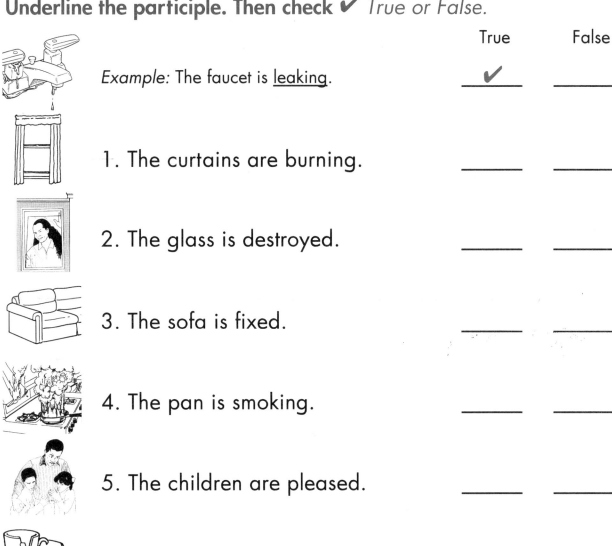

	True	False
Example: The faucet is <u>leaking</u>.	✔	
1. The curtains are burning.		
2. The glass is destroyed.		
3. The sofa is fixed.		
4. The pan is smoking.		
5. The children are pleased.		
6. The dishes are stained.		

Past Tense: Irregular Verbs

Present

I We You They	**do** the work. **go** home. **get** a new rug. **come** by car.
He She It	**does** the work. **goes** home. **gets** a new rug. **comes** by car.

Past

I We You They He She It	**did** the work. **went** home. **got** a new rug. **came** by car.

Underline the past tense verbs.

Example: Rita: Are you OK? I <u>went</u> to see Anita.

There <u>were</u> fire trucks in front of the building.

Fred: I know. We had a fire. Everybody got out fast. We are OK now. The fire started in the kitchen. My dinner burned. So did the curtains. But the building is OK.

Rita: You were lucky. Sometimes people are hurt in fires.

Write the past tense.

Example: Yesterday Fred __**went**__ to the store. He __**needed**__ new curtains.
                            (go)   (need)

1. Michael _____ trash barrels from Anita.
                  (get)

2. Carol _____ the kitchen floor.
           (wash)

3. They _____ to the Lins' apartment.
           (go)

4. They _____ the Lins clean their apartment.
           (help)

123456789 10 11 12
The Spice of Life ■ ■ ■ ■ ■ ■ ■ ■ ■

Planning a Meal
What's Anita doing?

Making a Grocery List

Check. ✔

	True	False
1. Anita is going to the supermarket.		
2. Carol wants 10 apples.		
3. Carol needs some flour.		
4. Anita doesn't have much cheese.		
5. Anita doesn't have many tomatoes.		
6. Anita doesn't need any chicken.		

Produce

 tomatoes $1.09/lb.

 baking apples 99¢/lb.

Meat, Seafood, Poultry

 fresh fish: haddock $4.99/lb.

 chicken breasts $1.99/lb.

Dairy Specials

 skim milk 89¢/quart

 premium orange juice $2.29   1/2 gal.

 Cheddar cheese $2.25/lb.

Bakery Buys

 fresh baked peach pie $3.29 each

 French bread 89¢/loaf

 dinner rolls $2.50/dozen

instant rice	macaroni	oatmeal
$1.89 28 oz. box	89¢ 15 oz. pkg.	$1.59 32 oz. box
coupon expires: 5/30/04	coupon expires: 5/30/04	coupon expires: 5/30/04

Fresh fish is expensive. It costs $4.99/lb.
Chicken is less expensive. It costs $1.99/lb.

Answer the questions.

1. What do you think is expensive in the ad?
2. What do you think isn't expensive in the ad?
3. What foods are expensive in your native country?

Down the Aisle

Match.

Aisle 1

Aisle 2

Aisle 3

Aisle 4

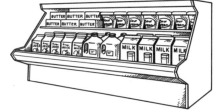

CARROTS $ .75/bunch   LETTUCE $1.09/each   BROCCOLI $1.09/bunch   ONIONS $1.69 5lb.bag   POTATOS $1.99 5lb.bag   TOMATOES $1.09/lb.   BANANAS $.69/lb.

SNOW PEAS $2.99/lb.

STRAWBERRIES $1.95 Pint

Complete the sentences.

1. Broccoli and _____ cost the same.

2. Onions and potatoes are sold in _____ bags.

3. _____ are sold by the pint.

4. A _____ of carrots costs 75¢.

5. Two pounds of bananas cost _____.

Answer the questions.

1. Can you think of some other fruits and vegetables?

2. What fruits and vegetables can you get in your native country?

Meat, Seafood, and Poultry

Check. ✔

	Chicken	Sausage	Fish
1. What costs more than $4.00?			
2. What costs less than $3.00?			
3. What is the cheapest per pound?			
4. What is the most expensive per pound?			
5. What weighs one pound?			

Choose the correct answer.

1. What fish is on sale?	*haddock*	*halibut*
2. Is the fish fresh or frozen?	*fresh*	*frozen*
3. Does Anita see the chicken in the case?	*yes*	*no*

Read Anita's shopping list.

milk   sugar
chicken   flour
butter   bread
carrots   cheese
rice   tortillas
lettuce   rolls
yogurt   muffins
apples
cookies

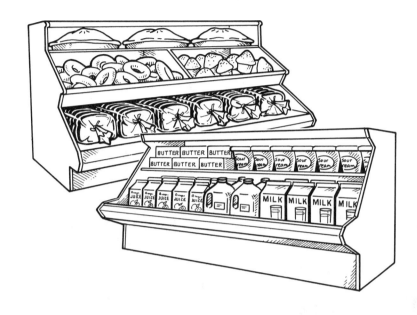

These foods are sold in the dairy department.
Underline what Anita needs to buy in the dairy department.

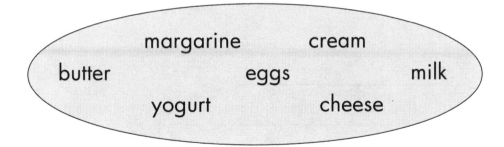

margarine   cream
butter   eggs   milk
yogurt   cheese

These foods are sold in the bakery department.
Underline what Anita needs to buy in the bakery department.

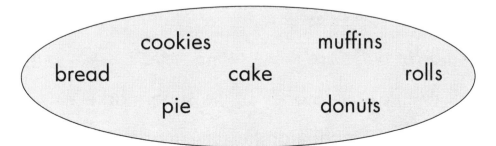

cookies   muffins
bread   cake   rolls
pie   donuts

At the Checkout

Complete the sentences.

Anita is buying ...

1. a gallon of _____.

2. a box of _____.

3. a quart of _____.

4. a bag of _____.

5. a loaf of _____.

6. a package of _____.

Answer the questions.

1. What kinds of bags are there at the store?

2. How does Anita save money at the supermarket?

3. How do you save money at the supermarket?

Anita invited some friends for dinner. She made chicken tacos. It's her favorite dish. Carol and Fred brought homemade apple pie for dessert. Joe brought fruit salad. He brought flowers for Anita too. Everyone enjoyed the dinner.

Answer the questions.

1. Do you enjoy having friends come to your home?

2. What do you make for your friends?

Favorite Foods

Interview.

What are your favorite foods?

Name	Fruit	Vegetable	Meat Seafood Poultry	Dessert
1. Anita	bananas	peas	chicken	apple pie
2.				
3.				
4.				
5.				

Make a meal with your favorite foods.

Vegetable	
Meat, Seafood, Poultry	
Dessert	
Fruit	

bakery   dairy   produce   meat, seafood, poultry

Cross out the food that doesn't belong.
Then write the correct food category.

1 | bread   onions   lettuce   tomatoes

_____

2 | eggs   bananas   strawberries   apples

_____

3 | milk   carrots   yogurt   cheese

_____

4 | beef   turkey   chicken   apples

_____

5 | muffins   cake   pie   cheese

_____

Count Nouns		Noncount Nouns
Singular	**Plural**	**Singular Only**
a banana	6 bananas	produce
an apple	a dozen apples	fruit

Look at the underlined words. Check ✔ *Count* or *Noncount*.

	Count	Noncount
Example: Anita needed some <u>apples</u>.	✔	
1. She found <u>poultry</u> in the first aisle.		
2. She also needed some <u>milk</u>.		
3. Anita paid with <u>cash</u>.		
4. She made 12 <u>tacos</u>.		
5. Joe brought <u>flowers</u> for Anita.		
6. He brought a <u>fruit salad</u>, too.		

Make two lists. Write *a, an* or *some*.

flour	sausages	✔bread	seafood	potatoes	meat
sugar	✔apple	orange	rice	sardines	chicken leg

Count	Noncount
an apple	some bread

Adjective	Comparative	Superlative
small	smaller	the smallest
comfortable	more comfortable	the most comfortable

Complete the sentences.

Example: Those shoes are the __**largest**__ pair in the store.
(large)

1. Richard is _____ than Janet.
(tall)

2. Michael is the _____ boy in his class.
(helpful)

3. This shirt is _____ than that one.
(colorful)

4. Lily is the _____ girl in her class.
(young)

Compare the bakery products. Make up sentences with comparatives and superlatives.

fresh baked peach pie
$3.29 each

French bread
89¢/loaf

dinner rolls
$2.50/dozen

Prepositions of Place

Preposition	Place	Preposition	Place
across	the room	on	the table
at	the post office	near	the bed
in	the kitchen	by	the door
next to	the bank	between	the books

This is Arturo's neighborhood.

Match.

1. Arturo lives in   a. the corner.

2. The supermarket is next to   b. Brooklyn.

3. The post office is on   c. the park.

4. The bank is near   d. the shoe store.

Complete the sentences.

1. The shoe store is _____ the supermarket and the drugstore.

2. The drugstore is _____ the street from the post office.

3. The children are _____ the park.

4. The bank is _____ the post office.

Singular			Plural			
I You	have/don't have		We You They		have/don't have	a sore leg.
He She It	has/doesn't have					

Complete the sentence with *have* or *has*.

1. Kendra _____ an earache.

2. Michael is sick too. He _____ the flu.

3. Fred says, "I think I'm getting sick. I _____ a sore throat."

4. Carol says, "We sure _____ a lot of problems this week."

Complete the sentences with *don't have* or *doesn't have*.

Carol is talking with her friend Rita.

1. "We _____ any aspirin. Can I get some from you?"

2. "Fred feels sick, but he _____ a fever."

3. "At least Michael _____ an earache like Kendra."

4. "I feel fine. I _____ any problems with my health."

| I
You
He
She
It | can/can't | go to school.

work full-time. |
| We
You
They | | speak Spanish. |

Example:

When **can** you **fix** the leak?   We **can fix** it tomorrow.

Can you **work** nights?   I **can't work** nights this week.

Complete the sentences with *can* or *can't*.

1. The sweater costs $24.95. Michael and Kendra
   have $12.00. They _____ buy the sweater.

2. The movie costs $7.00. Rita has $10.00.
   Rita _____ go to the movies.

3. Tom and May have $940. They need $200 for food.
   Their rent is $725. They _____ pay the rent.

Make up a sentence for each picture with *can* or *can't*.

	Singular	*Plural*
Count Noun	**a** letter **one** letter	**some** letters **two** letters **many** letters
Noncount Noun	mail	**some** mail **much** mail

Carol is teaching Kendra to bake chocolate chip cookies.
Kendra has a lot of questions.

Underline *how much* **or** *how many*.
Write the correct form of the noun.

Example:

bowl   "How much/<u>how many</u>   <u>bowls</u>   do I need?"

1. egg   "How much/how many _____ do I need?"

2. flour   "How much/how many _____ do I need?"

3. cup   "How much/how many _____ of sugar do I need?"

4. salt   "How much/how many _____ do I use?"

5. bag   "How much/how many _____ of chocolate chips
           do I put in?"

6. nuts   "How much/how many _____ do I need?"

Verbs: Verb + *to be* + Past Participle

I We You They	have	**to be**	help**ed**.
He She	wants	**to be**	help**ed**.
It	needs	**to be**	fix**ed**.

Complete the sentences with *to be*
and a form of the words below.

move	fix	clean	paint
call	cook	help	replace

Example: The curtains have <u>to be replaced</u>   .

1. The walls need _____.

2. The rugs have _____.

3. The window needs _____.

4. The landlord has _____.

5. Fred wants _____.

6. Dinner still needs _____.

7. The furniture has _____
   to another apartment.

Be	Present	Past
I	am	
He She It	is	was
We You They	are	were

Have	Present	Past
I	have	
He She It	has	had
We You They	have	

Complete the letter with *be* **or** *have.*

Dear Anita,

Richard and I ___are___ in Texas with Richard's family.

Yesterday, we _____ a birthday celebration for Richard

and his brother, Don. They _____ twins, you know. But

they _____ born on different days! Don _____ two

hours older. He _____ born late at night on July 8.

Richard _____ born early in the morning on July 9. So

every year they _____ a birthday party. It starts on one

day and ends on the next!

This _____ a great trip. Don _____ a comfortable

house. He _____ a lovely family, too. But we

_____ not used to such late hours. See you soon.

Janet

Write the past tense of the verbs.

Example: Rita _____**needed**_____ a job.
(need)

But she ____**didn't sign**____ the form.
(not sign)

The office ____**didn't call**____ her.
(not call)

1. Joe _____ work in a factory.
(start)

   But he _____ it.
   (not like)

   He _____ outdoor work.
   (want)

2. Anita _____ leaky faucets.
(fix)

   She _____ broken glass.
   (replace)

   She _____ to work in a store.
   (not want)

Complete each sentence with the past tense of the verb.

Example: Anita didn't **feel** good being far from her parents. She __*felt*__ lonely.

1. So she didn't **go** to Brooklyn. She _____ to Mexico.

2. Her parents didn't **get** her letter. They _____ her phone call.

3. Her mother didn't **make** a simple meal. She _____ a feast.

4. Anita didn't **do** the dishes. Her cousins _____ all the cleaning.

Write the questions. Put the words in the correct order.

Question	Answer
Example: __**What time is the party?**__ is/time/what/the party?	At 7 p.m.
1. _____ the party/is/when?	On Saturday.
2. _____ the Stevens' apartment/where/is?	At 63 South Street.
3. _____ going/is/to the party/who?	The family and some friends.
4. _____ invited/how many/friends/are?	About 10.

Read the problem. Then write a solution.
Use the words in the box or your own words.

clean	paint	repair	replace

Example: The dishes are broken.   You __**should replace**__ them.

1. The faucet is leaky.   Tom _____ it.

2. The Wilsons' furniture is burned.   They _____ it.

3. Tom and May's sofa is ripped.   They _____ it.

4. Kendra's bedroom walls are ruined.   Fred _____ and _____ them.

Adjectives: Demonstratives

Singular	Plural
This apple is good.	**These** apples are good.
That apple is bad.	**Those** apples are bad.

Match.

1. That bus is gone.

2. Those rolls are full price.

3. This bus goes to Roper Square.

4. These rolls are on sale.

a.

b.

c.

d.

States and Their Standard Postal Abbreviations

Alabama	AL	Montana	MT
Alaska	AK	Nebraska	NE
Arizona	AZ	Nevada	NV
Arkansas	AR	New Hampshire	NH
California	CA	New Jersey	NJ
Colorado	CO	New Mexico	NM
Connecticut	CT	New York	NY
Delaware	DE	North Carolina	NC
Florida	FL	North Dakota	ND
Georgia	GA	Ohio	OH
Hawaii	HI	Oklahoma	OK
Idaho	ID	Oregon	OR
Illinois	IL	Pennsylvania	PA
Indiana	IN	Rhode Island	RI
Iowa	IA	South Carolina	SC
Kansas	KS	South Dakota	SD
Kentucky	KY	Tennessee	TN
Louisiana	LA	Texas	TX
Maine	ME	Utah	UT
Maryland	MD	Vermont	VT
Massachusetts	MA	Virginia	VA
Michigan	MI	Washington	WA
Minnesota	MN	West Virginia	WV
Mississippi	MS	Wisconsin	WI
Missouri	MO	Wyoming	WY

Other Postal Abbreviations

District of Columbia	DC	United States	US
Puerto Rico	PR	United States of America	USA

The United States of America

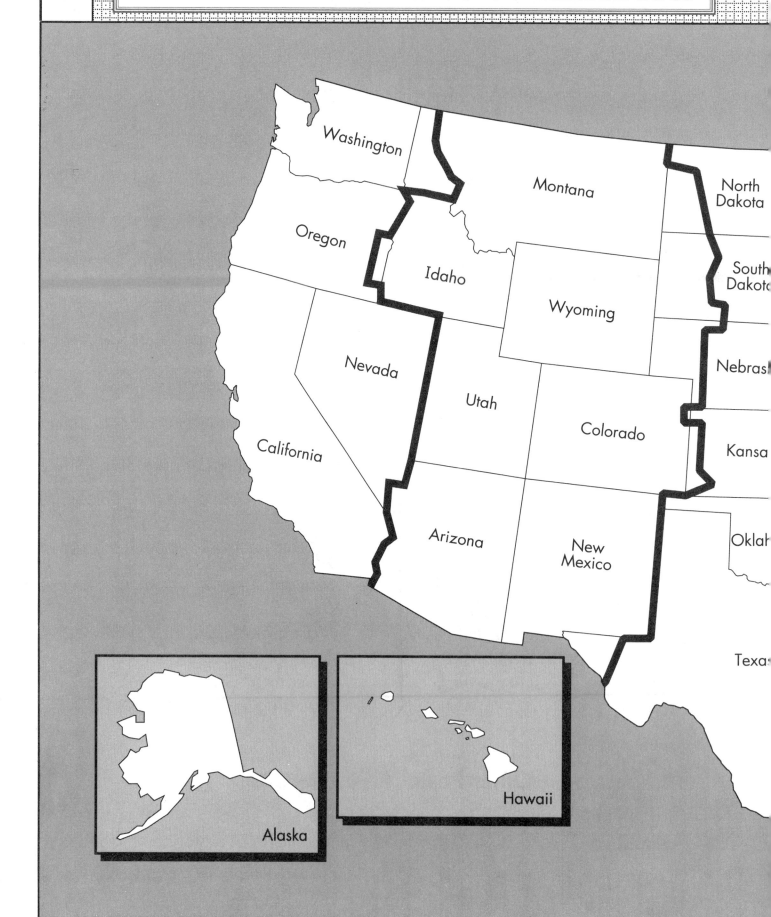

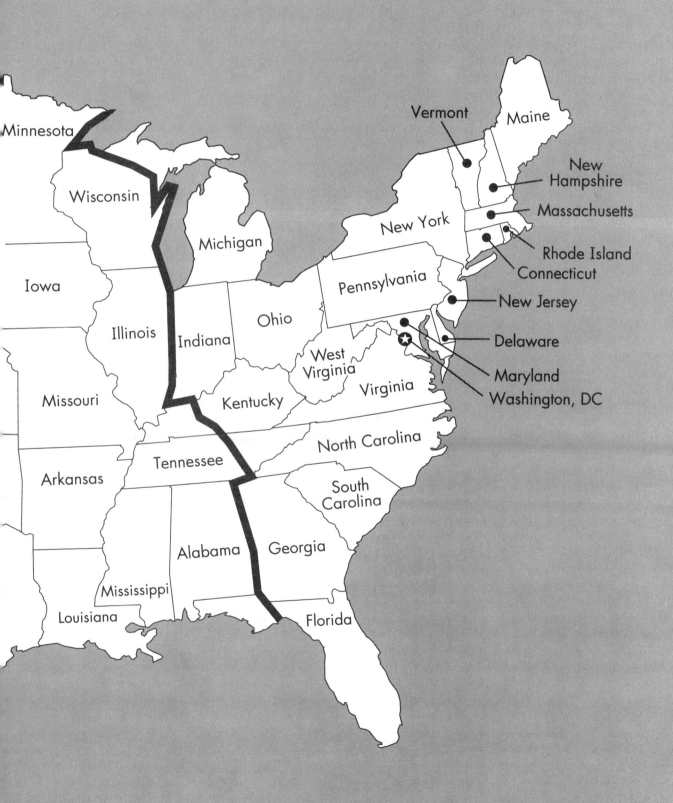

Minnesota

Wisconsin

Iowa

Michigan

Illinois

Indiana

Ohio

Missouri

Kentucky

West Virginia

Virginia

Arkansas

Tennessee

North Carolina

South Carolina

Alabama

Georgia

Mississippi

Louisiana

Florida

Vermont

Maine

New York

Pennsylvania

New Hampshire

Massachusetts

Rhode Island

Connecticut

New Jersey

Delaware

Maryland

Washington, DC

Common Abbreviations

Common Abbreviations in Addresses

Avenue....................Ave.
Boulevard ....Blvd.
Drive.......................Dr.
Lane ....Ln.
Place.......................Pl.
Road ....Rd.
Square ....Sq.
Street ....St.

Apartment...............Apt.

Post Office ....PO

Directions

East........................E
North ....N
South.......................S
West ....W
Northeast.................NE
Northwest ....NW
Southeast ....SE
Southwest ....SW

Time Periods

hour ....hr.
minute ....min.
second...................sec.
week ....wk.
month ....mo.
year ....yr.

a.m./AM: between midnight and noon

p.m./PM: between noon and midnight

Days of the Week

Sunday ....Sun./Su
Monday ....Mon./M
Tuesday ....Tues./Tu
Wednesday..............Wed./W
Thursday ....Thurs./Thu./Th
Friday.....................Fri./F
Saturday ....Sat./S

Months

January ....Jan.
February ....Feb.
March ....Mar.
April.......................Apr.
May ....—
June ....Jun.
July ....Jul.
August....................Aug.
September...............Sept.
October ....Oct.
November...............Nov.
December ....Dec.

Other Common Abbreviations

Company ....Co.
Incorporated ....Inc.
number ....no.